Top Dog

The Cocker Spaniel

by William R. Sanford and Carl R. Green

Edited by Julie Bach

CRESTWOOD HOUSE

New York
Collier Macmillan Canada
Toronto
Maxwell Macmillan International Publishing Group
New York   Oxford   Singapore   Sydney

Library of Congress Cataloging-in-Publication Data

Sanford, William R. (William Reynolds), 1927-
    The Cocker Spaniel / by William R. Sanford and Carl R. Green ; edited by Julie Bach.
    —1st ed.
        p.   cm. — (Top dog series)
        Summary: Discusses the history, physical characteristics, care, and breeding of the
    cocker spaniel.
        ISBN 0-89686-531-2
        1. Cocker spaniels—Juvenile literature.   [1. Cocker spaniels.   2. Dogs.]
    I. Green, Carl R.   II. Bach, Julie S., 1963-   III. Title.   IV. Series: Top dog
    (Crestwood House)
    SF429.C55S26   1990
    636.7'52—dc20
                                                                                    90-34059
                                                                                        CIP

PHOTO CREDITS

Cover: Reynolds Photography: (Larry Reynolds)
Jeff Heinzelman: 4
Kent and Donna Dannen: 6
Betsey O'Connor: (Dale Begany) 9, 25, 31, 43; (Diane
    Reid) 13, 34; (Linda Smith) 21; (Lloyd Alton) 22;
    (Ruth DeLomba) 33; (Missy Yuhl) 37
Animals Animals: (Michael Haricht) 11
Reynolds Photography: (Larry Reynolds) 14
Berg & Associates: (Margaret C. Berg) 17
Chandoha Photography: (Walter Chandoha) 27, 28
Peter Arnold, Inc.: (Gerard Lacz) 40

CRESTWOOD HOUSE

Macmillan Publishing Company
866 Third Avenue
New York, NY 10022

Collier Macmillan Canada, Inc.
1200 Eglinton Avenue East
Suite 200
Don Mills, Ontario M3C 3N1

Printed in the United States of America
First Edition
10 9 8 7 6 5 4 3 2 1

CONTENTS

For more information about cocker spaniels, write to:

American Spaniel Club
c/o Ms. Margaret M. Ciezkowski
12 Wood Lane South
Woodmere, NY 11598-2231

AN UNEXPECTED CHAMPION

Tom Clute, a Michigan salesman, was overjoyed when he saw his birthday present. The *purebred* cocker spaniel hadn't cost much because there were no champions in its family. But the little dog was full of energy and high spirits.

Tom named his new cocker Prince. They hit it off right away. Prince learned to shake hands and to roll over. Tom studied books on *obedience trials* and began training Prince for competition. The little cocker was soon winning prizes at local shows.

One of Tom's friends talked him into training the cocker for *field trials*. Tom had never hunted, and he knew nothing about tests of a dog's hunting abilities. But he read as much as he could, and then he started a training program. Prince had to learn to find game birds by scent. Then the dog had to retrieve the birds after they'd been shot.

When he went out on sales calls, Tom carried a crate of live pigeons in his car. Out in the

Because they make such lovable pets, cocker spaniels have become favorites with dog owners all over America.

countryside, he stopped and planted pigeons in the brush. Prince learned to find the birds and to *flush* them from their hiding places. It was harder for him to control his desire to chase the pigeons when they flew. In field trials, however, a dog must stand quietly until commanded to retrieve. Prince learned his lessons well.

Before long, the cocker was winning field trials all over the Midwest. The victories qualified him for the sport's biggest event, the Cocker National Championships. Tom wasn't sure about entering the New Jersey competition. After all, Prince had three strikes

To learn how to track well, a cocker needs lots of training.

against him already. No American cocker had ever won the event. No *amateur* handler had ever won. And no one from the Midwest had ever walked away with the trophy. It was Tom's mother who talked him into giving Prince a chance.

The competition was as tough as Tom had feared it would be. But Prince beat out one of the favorites on the first day. By the second day, Prince was the only amateur entry left in the trials. Tom could have settled for the amateur title. Instead, he decided to let Prince go all the way.

Only two dogs remained as the second day came to a close. One was an English cocker named Greatford Meadowcourt Pin. The other was Prince. Now it was time for the water test. Each dog was expected to retrieve a duck from a large pond.

The champion English cocker went first. The large crowd grew quiet as the judge waved a signal. A hunter shot the duck, which fell with a splash. Pin's handler ordered him to retrieve. The dog ran back and forth, building up his courage. The handler gave him a second command. This time Pin jumped into the cold water, swam to the duck and brought it back. The judges agreed that it was an excellent retrieve.

Prince was ready for his turn. When the duck fell, the cocker trembled with excitement. He could hardly wait for the command to go. When it came, he leaped 15 feet across the water and splashed down. The crowd gasped. Prince came up swimming and quickly retrieved the duck. People cheered and clapped as the dog laid the bird at Tom's feet. The little cocker had earned his place in dog history.

Tom Clute wasn't surprised that his birthday-present cocker had won a national championship. Prince's skill, courage, and lovable nature are all part of the *breed's* heritage.

THE HISTORY OF THE COCKER SPANIEL

Like all domestic dogs, cocker spaniels belong to the order *Carnivora* and the species *Canis familiaris*. They are meat-eating mammals, or *carnivores*. The gentle, playful cocker

The gentle, lovable cocker spaniel is also a great hunter.

spaniels you see in a pet store window come from a long line of hunters. In fact, spaniels were among the first dogs that early hunters trained to find and retrieve game.

Long before the invention of shotguns and hunting rifles, hunters used dogs and trained birds to capture small game. First they set a falcon or hawk free to circle in the sky. These birds of prey frightened the smaller game birds, which stayed hidden in the brush. Then the spaniel was turned loose to flush the birds out of their hiding places. The hunters captured the birds by throwing a large net over both the birds and the hunting dog.

For hundreds of years, all types of spaniels were grouped together. These dogs probably came from Spain, which is why they were given the name "spaniel." In the 17th century, spaniels were separated into two basic types. One type retrieved game from the water; the other retrieved game on land. Some of the larger land spaniels sprang on their prey. They became known as "springing" or "springer" spaniels. The smaller land spaniels could move easily through dense brush. They were especially good at hunting a game bird called the woodcock. They were called "cocker" spaniels.

For many years, springers and cockers were thought of as one breed. Springers and cockers could even come from the same *litter* of puppies. But in time, distinct breeds developed from these dogs.

In the 1880s, English cocker spaniels first appeared at dog shows in America. They were an instant success. Americans admired the dog's hunting ability, good looks, gentle nature, and small size. In time, American *breeders* set out to produce even smaller cockers. These small dogs became known as American cockers. The American Kennel Club (AKC) made the division official in 1946. English and American cocker spaniels were recognized as two separate breeds. Both are common in America. The only difference between them is size.

Very few people now think of cockers as hunting dogs. They have won a place in Americans' hearts because they make such lovable pets. In fact, the cocker is often called the most popular dog in America.

Since they first appeared in dog shows in the 1800s, cockers have grown steadily in popularity.

THE COCKER SPANIEL IN CLOSE-UP

The cocker spaniel is popular for good reason. It is a handsome, gentle dog that loves almost everyone it meets. Its sturdy body is strong enough for hunting, yet it is small enough to cuddle on your lap.

An adult cocker spaniel measures about 15 inches from the *withers* to the ground. It weighs between 23 and 28 pounds. Its body is strong and compact with a broad chest supported by straight, powerful legs. Like most hunting dogs, cockers can keep up a fast pace for hours at a time.

The cocker's back slopes gently to its tail, which is usually docked. *Docking* means that breeders cut off the first or second joint of the tail when the cocker puppy is a few days old. The puppy doesn't feel much pain, and the stub heals quickly. If you plan to show your dog, the AKC requires that its tail be docked. Some breeders would like to get rid of this rule. It began when cockers were used in hunting. Hunters worried that the dog's long, feathery

The feathered look of the cocker spaniel's coat gives it an elegant appearance.

tail might get caught in thick underbrush. Docking the tail, they thought, would make the cocker a more efficient hunting dog.

A cocker's long, soft, silky coat is truly beautiful. On some dogs, the outer coat lies flat, but many cockers have wavy hair. The long hair that grows on the ears, chest, underbody, and legs gives the dog a feathered look. Some cockers look as though they are wearing fringed, floor-length skirts.

You can find cockers in many different colors. The most common colors are black, reddish brown, *buff*, white, golden brown, or tan. Parti-colored cockers have coats that are two different colors—tan and white, for example.

A cocker's head is well rounded, the *muzzle* square. The strong jaw and teeth are those of a hunter and retriever. The cocker also has noticeable eyebrows above large, dark eyes. The slightly almond-shaped eyes hold a look that seems to say, "I'll do whatever I can to make you love me." The cocker's ears are one of its most notable features. Set low on its head, the ears are long and silky. In fact, some cockers have ears so long that they fall into the dogs' food dishes. This causes problems at dog shows. Some owners tie their cockers' ears in *snoods* made from stockings. The snoods keep the ears clean until the dogs enter the show ring.

A purebred cocker is a beautiful, well-proportioned dog. Few people can resist its good looks and friendly, gentle personality. Many owners, however, forget that their cockers still have the keen senses of an all-around hunting dog.

Cocker spaniels come in many colors, including black, white, tan, and combinations of different shades.

THE COCKER SPANIEL'S SENSES

A cocker spaniel's senses are adapted for what it was bred to do—hunt. Cockers have ears, eyes, noses, and tongues as humans do, but their sense organs work differently. For example, dogs don't see colors the way people do, but they see better in the dark. They also see movement in the distance better than people do. Their special ways of seeing help them locate game birds when they're hunting.

Because dogs are often bounding through dusty fields or thick underbush, they have a third eyelid, called the *haw*. The haw sweeps away dust and grit that blow into the eye. It is mostly hidden, but you can see a little of it in the corner of the eye close to the nose. The haw is most visible when a dog is tired.

Dogs have a much better sense of hearing than people do. They can hear sounds that are too high pitched for humans to hear. They can also pick up sounds four times farther away. However, a floppy-eared dog like the cocker can't hear distant sounds as well as a dog with erect, pointed ears. This weakness may have been bred into some hunting dogs. Breeders wanted the dogs to rely on sight and smell. If their hearing was too good, they might be distracted by distant sounds.

The cocker spaniel's nose is also keener than a human nose. Experts say that it's up to a million times more sensitive. The human nose has about one-half square inch of *olfactory area*. This area contains the nerve endings that are sensitive to smells. The dog's olfactory area averages 21 square inches! The area is folded over inside the nose, creating a series of ridges that trap smells.

Cocker spaniels receive information about the world around them by smell.

Cockers sniff at everything around them. This is how they get most of their information. Because they can discover so much through their noses, they can be trained to locate game, drugs, bombs, and lost children. Cockers have even saved lives by alerting their owners when they smelled gas or smoke.

Cockers' brains are too small for logical, human thought. But they often seem to understand what is going on around them. While a cocker may not know the words you use, it can pick up your tone of voice and your body language. Dogs do not reason, but they are capable of learning, which makes training possible. Most dogs want very much to please their owners. This trait makes them easier to train than most other animals. You'll find that a cocker spaniel is an especially intelligent people-pleaser.

A WINNING PERSONALITY

Do you like dogs that wiggle with joy when you walk in the door? If you do, a cocker's right for you. The cocker wiggle delights everyone who is around this breed for long.

Cockers fit perfectly into most families. They are gentle and loving, playful and carefree. Owners call them the sweetheart of dogs. At dog shows, they often get more applause than other breeds. Their personalities—not just their looks—win the hearts of many fans.

Some of the cocker's character comes from its breeding as a hunter. Like all hunting dogs, it is brave, alert, and hard working. But for all its love of the chase, it is not aggressive. The cocker is actually quite gentle. This makes it a good pet for families with children. Although it needs exercise and prefers the country, it adjusts well to a city apartment.

A cocker spaniel quickly accepts its owner as boss and gives back great loyalty and affection. It enjoys being trained and seems to take pleasure in obeying. But a cocker doesn't like being left alone. It will be unhappy if it isn't taken on family outings.

Because cockers have long been so popular, a few breeders tried to produce more dogs to sell. In their hurry, they mated poor-quality males and females. Poor breeding affected the personalities of some of the puppies. Unlike well-bred cockers, they were noisy, nervous, and unhealthy. Sadly, some of these poor-quality dogs gave birth to their own litters. Their puppies were just as hard to live with as the parents had been.

The faults of a few nervous dogs should not be held against all cockers. A carefully bred cocker is a playful, loving pet. It has certainly lost some of the toughness of the hunter. But it still shows the energy, intelligence, and willingness to work that its ancestors had.

CHOOSING A COCKER SPANIEL

Once you know you want a cocker spaniel, how do you choose the right one?

First, decide on the type of cocker you want. Do you want a winner at dog shows, or a wonderful pet? A dog that will win blue ribbons can cost $500 or more. A pet-quality dog will cost $400 or less.

A breeder is the best person from whom to buy cocker puppies. If you buy a purebred, the seller will give you the puppy's *pedigree*. These papers list the puppy's ancestors and allow you to register the dog with the AKC. To register your puppy, you will need a form signed by the breeder. Then you must pick a name for your new pet. The AKC limits each

Careful breeding will produce beautiful cockers like the black and tan dogs shown here.

name to 25 letters or less. After you send in your application and fee, you'll receive your dog's personal certificate of registration. Registering a dog protects its value and the value of any puppies it produces later on.

Choosing a male or female cocker spaniel depends mostly on whether you want to raise puppies. If you don't want to breed your female, your *veterinarian* can *spay* her. This simple operation prevents your dog from ever getting pregnant. It costs about $100. You can

21

also make sure your male dog doesn't make another dog pregnant. Your vet can *neuter* him. That operation costs about the same as spaying.

Otherwise, males and females both make good pets. A male tends to roam more, but a female comes in *heat* twice a year when she's ready to mate. If you don't want *crossbreed* puppies, you'll have to keep your female locked up when she is in heat.

The most important rule when choosing a puppy is to pick a healthy one. The puppy should be alert, active, and bright-eyed. Check

This playful cocker rides along with its owner as he cuts the grass.

to see if its skin and ears are clean. Avoid puppies that are too fat or too thin, too shy or too aggressive. If you can, take a look at the puppy's parents. If they're sturdy, good-natured dogs, the puppy will probably grow up to be like them.

It's also a good idea to take the puppy to a veterinarian for a checkup before the sale is final. Sellers will often give you eight hours to do this. Just be sure that your agreement with the seller is clear.

Finally, do some research ahead of time. Learn as much as you can about cocker spaniels. It doesn't matter whether you want a champion or just a good pal. Experts say the more you know about cockers before you buy one, the better chance you'll have of picking the right dog.

TRAINING YOUR COCKER SPANIEL

When you begin to train your cocker, remember that it doesn't understand human speech. It helps to keep your language simple. You can use any word for a command. Just be sure you use the same one every time. One trainer used reversed commands to create a "trick" dog for the movies. The dog was taught to sit on the command "Up!" and to come on the command "Stay!" The dog didn't know that the words meant something else to the movie audience. It only knew there would be a reward for performing the actions the trainer expected.

Cockers need kindness and attention. They'll respond very well to praise and pats on the head during training. Of course, a dog biscuit helps, too! You'll find that rewards work much better than punishment.

Your first training task is to *housebreak* your puppy. This takes patience, the key to all dog training. Take the puppy outside frequently, especially after meals. Be alert when it starts sniffing or circling a spot on the floor. These are signs for you to move fast! Keep the puppy outdoors until it has relieved itself, then praise it. When the puppy has an accident inside, scolding won't help unless you do it right after the accident. After about three seconds, the dog won't understand why it is being punished.

After housebreaking your cocker, teach it some simple commands. First, teach your puppy to come when you call. Always treat your puppy well when it does come to you. If it

Cocker spaniel puppies will learn quickly if given a lot of attention and kindness.

must be scolded, go to the puppy. Never call a puppy to you and then punish it.

Some other useful commands a cocker can learn early are "Heel," "Sit," and "Stay." *Heeling* means your dog walks at your side, adjusts to your speed, and stops when you stop. When you train, use a leash and *choke collar*. The collar doesn't really choke the dog, but it does tighten when the dog strains at the leash. The dog learns to connect a tight collar with a mistake. It's okay to use an angry tone of voice to scold your dog, but don't shout. Learning to control your own temper is the first step toward controlling your cocker.

The list of things a cocker can learn is almost endless. The dog can learn to roll over, to stay off your dad's chair, and not to jump up on Aunt Eileen. Your best tools are patience and rewards. If you have to say "No!" say it firmly and sharply. Repeat the lessons over and over until the dog learns them perfectly. When your cocker does something right, praise it and give it a bit of dog biscuit. Before long, everyone you meet will say, "What a wonderful dog!" That's when you'll know that the hours of hard work were worthwhile.

CARING FOR YOUR COCKER SPANIEL

A cocker spaniel is fun to own. But it also needs constant care. Your dog depends on you for food, shelter, health care, *grooming*, and exercise.

When you buy your puppy, find out what it has been eating and continue that diet. A small puppy needs four or five small meals a day. By six months, it will need only two larger meals a day. By one year, a single evening feeding will be enough.

Always give your dog high-quality, fresh food. Feed it at the same time every day, and take away any uneaten food. When you buy a canned or dry dog food, read the label. Look for a brand with lots of protein.

A dog needs its own bed. You can buy an expensive dog bed at a pet store. But a puppy

Good grooming and a balanced diet will produce healthy, good-looking cockers.

will be just as happy with a cardboard box with some newspapers and an old blanket. The box must be big enough to give your pet room to stretch.

When you first bring your puppy home, you might be in for some sleepless nights. A new puppy cries because it's lonely. Up until now, it could snuggle up to its mother and the other puppies in the litter. You may be tempted to let it sleep with you, but don't give in! Your dog must learn to sleep by itself. Putting a hot water bottle in the bed, along with an old doll for company, can help. Sometimes the ticking of a wind-up clock can comfort an unhappy puppy, too.

It's important to find a good veterinarian for your dog right away. The vet will make sure that the dog has had its shots. These shots can prevent deadly diseases such as *distemper*. Try to be alert to changes in your dog's looks and behavior. Whenever something doesn't seem quite right, the vet should check it out.

Cockers need plenty of exercise. Walking, running, and playing together will keep both you and your dog healthy. Give your dog a hard rubber ball to play with. It will also enjoy a big beef rib bone with no harmful splinters. Chewing on the bone will exercise its jaws and keep its teeth clean.

With the proper care, cocker spaniels will live long, happy lives.

Your dog will begin to lose its puppy coat at about eight months. From then on, it needs to be brushed every day. If a dog isn't groomed, its beautiful coat will become matted and tangled. Pay special attention to your cocker's ears. They are sometimes trouble spots. Don't poke deeply into the ears, but clean the areas you can reach. A wad of cotton dipped in warm, soapy water will do the job safely.

The more time you spend caring for your dog, the happier you both will be. Dogs are just like people. They thrive when they are loved and well cared for.

BREEDING YOUR COCKER SPANIEL

Letting your female cocker spaniel have puppies can be an exciting experience. But good breeding requires careful planning. Too many crossbreed puppies end up in animal shelters because no one wants them. It's up to you to make sure that your purebred cocker has strong, healthy puppies. If all goes well, you may be able to sell the puppies for a profit.

When breeding your cocker, it is important to make sure that your dog is in good health.

First, it's important to make sure the female, or *bitch*, is fully mature before she is mated. Her first heat will probably occur when she is six to eight months old. But at that age, she is still growing. Her bones will not be fully developed until she is about a year old. After that, she has a much better chance of having healthy, full-sized puppies.

Choosing the father, or *stud*, is the next important step. If you plan to sell the puppies, choose a stud registered with the AKC. If you bought your cocker from a kennel, ask the

31

breeder for a suitable mate for your dog. A veterinarian can also help you locate a quality stud dog.

Make sure your bitch is in good physical condition and has had all her shots. This is important to the stud's owner. You can pay the stud fee in cash or with "the pick of the litter." That means giving the best puppy to the owner.

About 10 or 12 days after a female comes into heat, she should be taken to the stud. The stud's owner will supervise the mating. Once a bitch is pregnant, she has to be kept away from other male dogs. If she mates again, her litter could have puppies by two different fathers.

A cocker's pregnancy lasts about 63 days. It's best to give her extra protein during this time. She will need regular but gentle exercise and several small meals a day. Having puppies is natural for a female. But like most mothers-to-be, she will welcome extra care and attention.

A LITTER OF PUPPIES

When a dog gives birth, she usually handles matters on her own. Be ready, though, to help

This cocker spaniel mother had both black-and-white and brown-and-white puppies in the same litter.

in case she needs it. If her labor goes on for too long without results, for example, you may have to call in the vet.

Cockers usually have litters of three to five puppies. Most of the puppies arrive about half an hour apart. When a newborn arrives, the mother first licks it. The licking removes the birth sac and starts the puppy's breathing. The mother also bites off the *umbilical cord*. After all the puppies are born, the female nudges them into position to find her *teats*. The puppies' sucking helps her produce the rich milk they need.

For the first weeks of their lives, puppies do little more than eat and sleep. The mother provides the two things they need most: food and warmth.

Careful breeders never let newborn puppies get cold. Their birth coat isn't thick enough to protect them. Two-week-old puppies can go outside unless the weather is very cold. A romp in the sunshine is good for them. The puppies'

When cocker puppies are born, their eyes are closed. It takes about two weeks for them to open.

eyes open at about this time. At four weeks they can see and hear quite well.

You can add soft foods to a cocker puppy's diet about the third week. Easy-to-eat foods such as cereal and cow's milk are good choices. Some time between the fourth and sixth weeks the puppies can be *weaned* from their mother. They should begin to eat chopped raw meat and soft dog food. Also, offer them water several times a day.

People often forget that young puppies have fragile bones and a "soft spot" on their skulls. A blow to this spot can damage a puppy's brain. Ask everyone to be careful when they pick up your puppies. In fact, puppies do better when they are not handled too much. They need lots of naps because they tire easily. In addition, too much excitement can keep them from digesting their food. Let the puppies decide when it's time for play.

Even though you may want to keep the puppies, you probably don't have room for four or five cockers. The puppies can go to their new homes when they are seven or eight weeks old.

THE STAR OF THE SHOW

How do you know if your cocker has the qualities of a champion? Measure it against the AKC standards for cockers. If you think your dog compares well, enter it in competition.

Most people begin by entering a "match show." A match show gives newcomers a chance to practice showing their dogs. These shows are similar to more advanced ones, but no points are awarded. If your dog does well in match shows, it is probably ready for real competition.

Upcoming dog shows are listed in newspapers and in dog magazines. Send for an entry form, fill it in carefully, and mail it back with the entry fee.

You can enter your dog in one of the five official show classes. Perhaps it will start out in Puppy Class, which is for dogs between six and twelve months old. Another good choice is Novice Class, which is for dogs more than six months old that have never won a first prize. American-bred Class is for dogs more than six months old and born in the United States. Bred-by-exhibitor Class is for dogs being shown by their breeders. Competition is toughest in Open Class, which attracts all dogs six months old or more. In this class, a dog has to compete against the current champions.

To train your dog for competition, teach it to trot beside you, keeping its head up. In the show ring, you'll have to *gait* the dog in front of judges who will watch its form. Your dog will also have to stand still and allow the judges to examine it. They'll look your dog over from head to rump, and they may look in its mouth to check its teeth. Practice every step in the

This beautiful dog worked very hard to win Best in Show.

SANTA MARIA K.C. 1988

judging many times so that your dog won't be nervous when handled by strangers.

If you've kept your dog well groomed, it will need only touch-up grooming on the day of the show. A professional groomer can show you how to make the dog look its best.

It's better not to feed a dog before the start of the show. The dog will feel and look peppier if it hasn't eaten a big meal. Settle your dog down and wait for the judges to call its class. When the time comes, you and your dog take center stage. Will all your work pay off? If it does, you'll have the thrill of seeing your cocker spaniel selected as Best of Breed or even Best in Show.

MARKING ITS TERRITORY

Anyone who walks a male cocker spaniel knows the routine. The dog stops at a bush or post, lifts a hind leg, and urinates. It trots a few yards and stops again. A few yards farther on it stops again. The behavior is so common that people hardly notice it.

Scientists describe this practice as *scent*

marking. It starts when male dogs reach sexual maturity at about five months. When they stop to leave their scent on a tree, they release only a small amount of urine. In this way, each dog can spread its scent over a large area.

Scent marking has two purposes. First, it creates a trail that other dogs can follow. More importantly, the splashes of urine serve as boundary markers. The habit of marking territory started with the dog's wild ancestors. These wolflike dogs marked the territory around their dens in the same way. This warned other wild dogs that the area was occupied. Any strange dog that ventured into the territory was certain to be attacked.

Today's cocker spaniels haven't lost their ancient *instincts.* The need to mark their territory still runs strong. Instead of a hunting territory, the males mark the area around their owners' homes. Some will attack any dog that strays into that territory. Others accept the local dogs into their "pack."

Young cockers learn by experience. If a six-month-old male finds an open gate, he'll wander through it, sniffing along. The scent markers left by other dogs don't mean much to him. But the young male soon discovers his mistake. Older dogs bark savagely and drive him away. After several days, the puppy learns

to respect the scent markings. At the same time, he begins to mark his own territory.

An older cocker spaniel isn't as easily frightened. He may use his own scent to cover up another dog's scent, challenging that dog's territory. First he sniffs at a scent marker left on a tree. Then he cocks his leg, splashes the tree, and trots off happily. Thanks to fences and leash laws, the cocker is rarely forced to fight to back up his challenge.

◣A SMART DOG

Dogs sometimes surprise people with how smart they are. Take a reddish brown cocker named Penny, for example. Penny lived on a large family farm. During the summer, Penny joined the children on their daily trip to a nearby swimming hole. Penny dog-paddled like the natural swimmer she was and happily retrieved the sticks the children threw.

When fall and winter came, Penny stayed close to home. Her bed was in a small shed next to the henhouse. She kept watch over the chickens and barked furiously whenever strangers approached. Sometimes on cold nights, she curled up in front of the fire in the farmhouse.

Cockers are curious dogs that like to explore their surroundings.

One spring the family decided they wanted Penny to have puppies. They bred her to a male cocker that lived three farms away. As the weeks passed, Penny's abdomen began to swell. It was obvious that she was going to be a mother.

In the middle of July, Penny gave birth to four fat puppies. The puppies were healthy, but the weather was terribly hot. The family worried about Penny and her litter. The *whelping box* was kept in the shed, which felt like the inside of an oven. The children took turns keeping plenty of cool water in Penny's large water dish.

One afternoon one of the children stopped at the shed to check on the puppies. A quick look showed that all of them were soaking wet! Certain that something was wrong, the boy ran back to the house to get his mother.

Together they hurried to the shed. The woman saw at once that the puppies looked healthy enough. As they watched, Penny picked up one of the puppies in her mouth and carried it gently to the water dish. She dunked it in the water several times and then returned it to the box. One by one she did the same thing with each of the other three puppies. Then Penny dipped her own paws in the dish. When she saw her audience, she wagged her tail.

Murphy, the cocker spaniel in this picture, doesn't look too happy about being one of Santa's reindeer.

The family talked about Penny's clever behavior at dinner that night. The children decided that she must have remembered those days at the swimming hole. Clearly, she couldn't take her puppies there to cool them off. With only the water dish available, she'd done the next best thing. Like many cocker spaniels, Penny proved to be a very smart dog.

GLOSSARY/ INDEX

Amateur 7—One who is not a professional but competes as a hobby.

Bitch 31, 32—An adult female dog.

Breed 8, 10, 11—A particular type of dog with common ancestors and similar characteristics. The cocker spaniel is one breed of dog.

Breeders 10, 17, 19, 20, 34, 36—People who raise and sell animals.

Buff 15—A yellowish brown color.

Carnivores 8—Meat-eating animals.

Choke Collar 25—A lead made from heavy metal links, which is used in training a dog.

Crossbreed 22, 30—A dog whose parents are different breeds.

Distemper 29—A viral disease that young dogs can get.

Docking 12, 13—Cutting off the first or second joint of a puppy's tail when the dog is a few days old.

Field Trials 5, 6—Contests to show how well dogs can hunt.

Flush 6, 9—To scare birds and other game out of their hiding places in fields or brush.

Gait 37—The movements of a dog's feet when it is walking, trotting, or running.

Grooming 26, 38—Bathing and brushing a dog to keep its coat clean and smooth.

Haw 16—An extra eyelid that helps protect a dog's eye.

Heat 22, 31—The days when a bitch is ready to mate.

Heeling 25—When a dog walks obediently at its owner's side.

Housebreak 24—To teach a dog to relieve itself on newspaper or outside the house.

Instincts 39—Natural behaviors that are inborn in a dog.

Litter 10, 32, 33—A family of puppies born at a single whelping.

Muzzle 15—The jaws, nose, and mouth of a dog.

Neuter 22—To operate on a male dog so he can't make a female dog pregnant.

Obedience Trials 5—Contests to show how well dogs have been trained.

Olfactory Area 17—The nerve endings inside the nose that sense odors.

Pedigree 20—A chart that lists a dog's ancestors.

Purebred 5, 20, 30—A dog whose ancestors were all of the same breed.

Scent Marking 38, 39, 41—A male dog's practice of urinating to mark his territory.

Snoods 15—Bags or caps placed on cockers' heads to keep their ears from falling into their food while they eat.

Spay 21—To remove a female dog's ovaries so she can't get pregnant.

Stud 31, 32—A purebred male used for breeding.

Teats 34—A female dog's nipples. Puppies suck on the teats to get milk.

Umbilical Cord 33—A hollow tube that carries nutrients to a puppy while it is in its mother's body.

Veterinarian 21, 23, 29, 32, 33—A doctor trained to take care of animals.

Weaned 35—Made a puppy stop drinking its mother's milk and eat solid food instead.

Whelping Box 42—A box in which a female dog can give birth to her puppies.

Withers 12—A dog's shoulders; the point where its neck joins the body. A dog's height is measured at the withers.